Ladybird Picture Books
Indoor Things
Outdoor Things
Things That Go
Things to Wear
Things to Play With

LADYBIRD BOOKS, INC.
Auburn, Maine 04210 U.S.A.
© LADYBIRD BOOKS LTD MCMLXXXVIII
Loughborough, Leicestershire, England

Printed in England

Things to Wear

Illustrated by **Marika Hahn**

Ladybird Books

red

sweater

boots

coat

scarf

orange

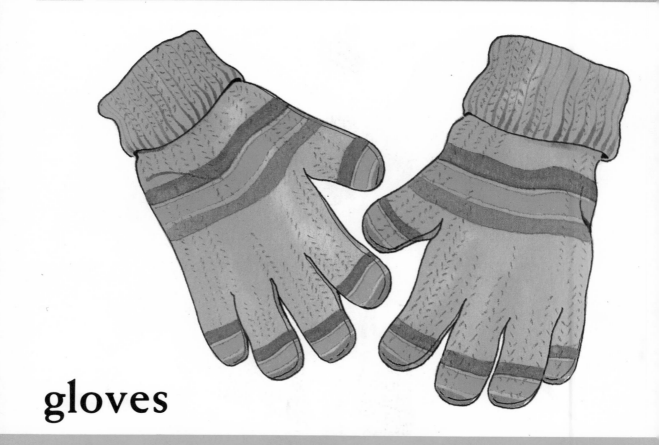

gloves

shirt

bathrobe

pajamas

yellow

dress

swimsuit

T-shirt

raincoat

green

skirt

pants

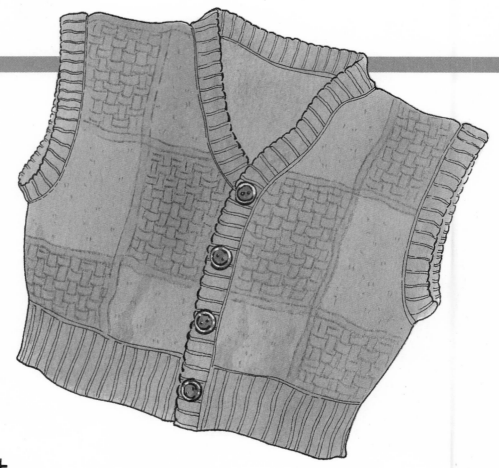

vest

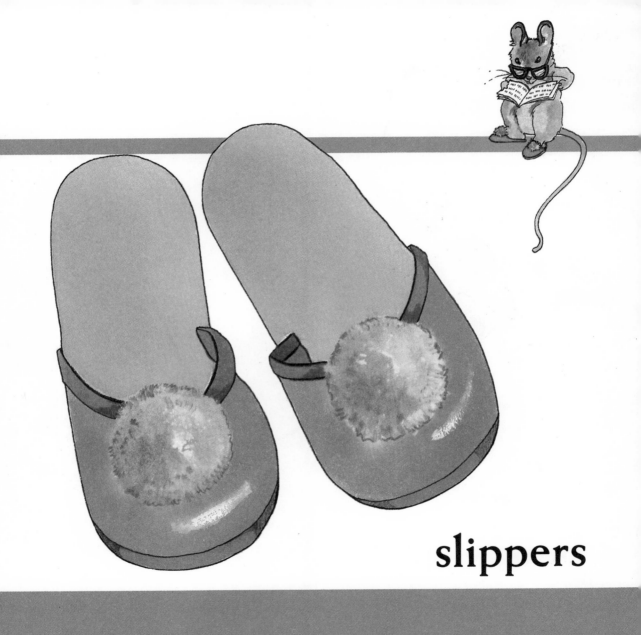

slippers

blue

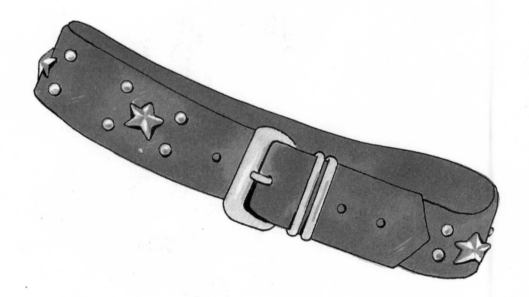

belt

jacket

shoes

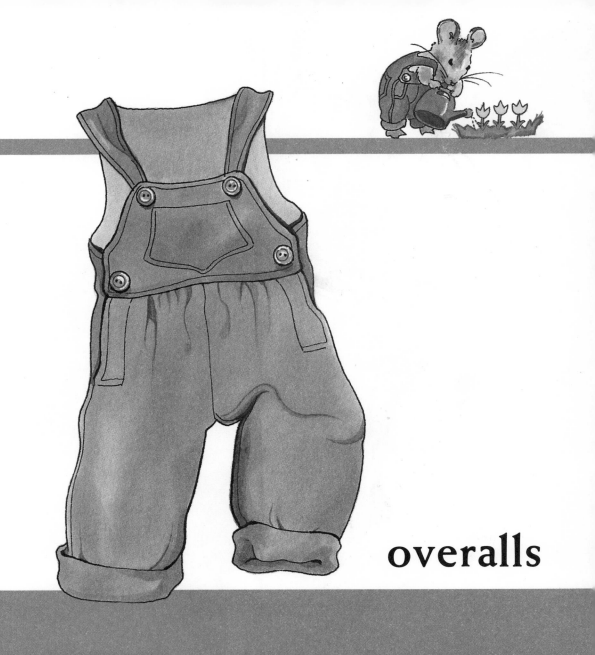

overalls

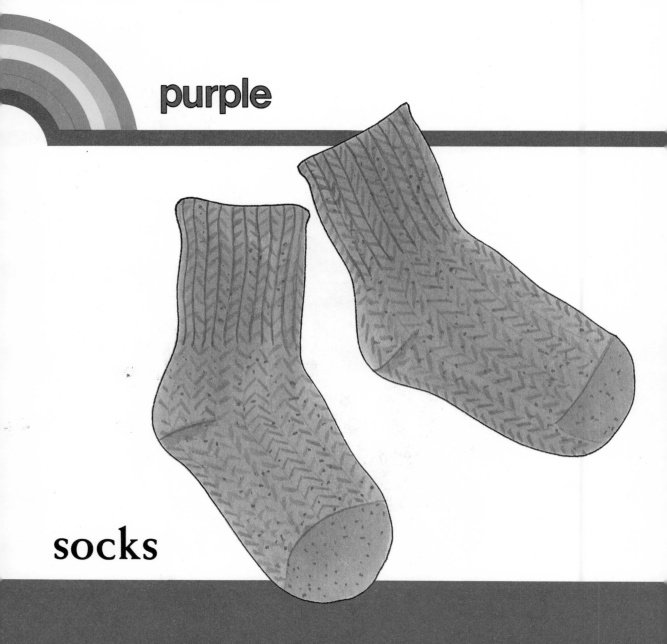

purple

socks

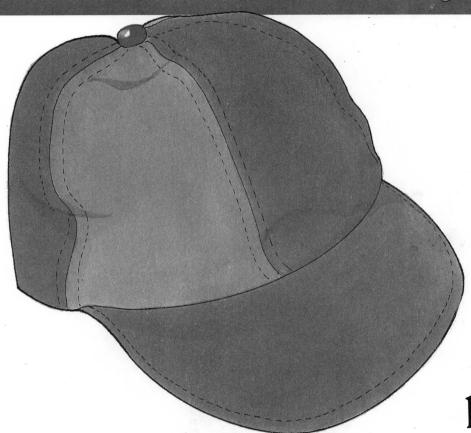

hat

tie

sweatsuit